M000160080

PENELOPE'S SUPERPOWER

by Melinda M. Cropsey

illustrated by Giada Rose

Copyright © 2018 by Breadcrumbs Publishing, a division of Breadcrumbs, LLC, Longmeadow, MA

All rights reserved. This book or any portion thereof may not be reproduced or used in any manner whatsoever without the express written permission of the publisher except for the use of brief quotations in a book review. Printed in the United States of America.

ISBN: 978-0-692-14348-3

For Garrett, Hal and Hunter

My name is Penelope.

I am a gift

from the stars...

and you are too!

My heart knows

what makes me special...

and yours does too!

I can connect to my heart.

It's easy...

and you can too!

I place my hands on my heart

and a smile on my face.

I imagine
that I am

in my quiet, happy place.

I breathe in like a flower...

and out like a shower.

I breathe in like a flower...

and out like a shower.

I breathe in like a flower...

and out like a shower.

And "POOF!"

I'm connected to my superpower.

With love, there is nothing

that I cannot do.

The same is true for you!

The world will be
a better place

because of you and me.

I am a rainbow of possibility...

and you are too!

More About Heart-Centered Breathing

Penelope's simple, heart-centered breathing practice offers children and adults alike a surprisingly powerful tool for calming, reducing stress, self-soothing and connecting to the wisdom of the heart!

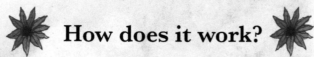 ## How does it work?

"I place my hands on my heart" - This gentle touch shifts focus from the head to the area around the heart and triggers the body's relaxation response: A collection of neurons known as the "tiny brain of the heart," send a message from the heart to the brain that you are peaceful and safe; the brain responds by producing oxytocin—the love hormone; and the oxytocin floods the body with positive feelings.

"… and a smile on my face." - Smiling reinforces and amplifies positive, core heart feelings of love, gratitude and appreciation. Purposefully smiling increases happiness and reduces stress.

"I imagine that I'm in my quiet, happy place." - Inviting a child to recall a place where they have felt happy, peaceful, safe, protected and loved evokes a host of positive feeling memories. Teaching a child that they have the power to re-experience those wonderful feelings, at will, is both soothing and empowering.

"I breathe in like a flower and out like a shower" - Consciously slowed breathing: Inhaling, as if you are drinking in the smell of a beautiful flower, is another means of sending your brain the message that you are peaceful and safe. Exhaling, out like a shower, while imagining bathing in the energy of warm, positive core heart feelings, is deeply calming and relaxing.

"and 'Poof' I'm connected to my Superpower!" - "Heart Intelligence" is defined as the flow of awareness and insight that is experienced when the mind and emotions are brought into balance and coherence through a self-initiated process.* Heart Intelligence manifests in intuitive thoughts and emotions that are beneficial to ourselves and others… in a word: LOVE!

Please join children, throughout the day, in taking time to connect to the Superpower of Love!

* Childre and Martin, (1999). *The HeartMath Solution*, HarperCollins Publishers, New York, NY, p.6.

About the Author

Melinda Cropsey is the founder of Breadcrumbs, LLC and the author of the Breadcrumbs Social-Emotional Curriculum. This unique curriculum, designed for children between the ages of 3-7, is rooted in her philosophy that the heart is the seat of emotional intelligence. She believes that by teaching children to tap into and celebrate their heart's innate capacities for love, compassion, empathy, kindness, gratitude and peace, they will come to understand and trust their hearts as an alternative source of wisdom within their bodies—the Treasure in their Chest!

Melinda is also the author of *A Quiet, Happy Place: A Children's Introduction to the Labyrinth*. She lives with her husband Henry in Longmeadow, MA.

About the Illustrator

Giada Rose is a freelance artist, graphic designer and handcrafter whose work includes everything from tarot decks to children's books. She is also the illustrator of *Penelope Hears Her Heart* by Katherine and Maya Ward and *Giants in the Clouds* by Maria Muscarella, and she sells her own prints and originals through her Etsy shop, Rosewitchery Handcrafts. You can see more of her work on her website, www.giada-rose.com.

CPSIA information can be obtained
at www.ICGtesting.com
Printed in the USA
LVHW070904280720
661632LV00022B/441

* 9 7 8 0 6 9 2 1 4 3 4 8 3 *